CHILDREN'S BIBLE STORIES WORKBOOK

STORIES FROM THE NEW TESTAMENT

SECOND EDITION REVISED

CLAUDETTE FRANCIS

authorHOUSE®

AuthorHouse™ LLC
1663 Liberty Drive
Bloomington, IN 47403
www.authorhouse.com
Phone: 1-800-839-8640

Cover Painting by Barbara Richardson

Published by AuthorHouse   08/09/2013

ISBN: 978-1-4817-2729-7 (sc)
ISBN: 978-1-4817-2730-3 (e)

This book is printed on acid-free paper.

Claudette Francis
4-170 Brickworks Lane
Toronto, Ontario, Canada
M6N 5H7
Tel: 647 884 4674
Email: claudettefrncs@yahoo.ca

HOW TO USE THIS BOOK

This book contains thirty-one (31) stories and each story has five parts.

1st   A NEW TESTAMENT STORY

The story is taken directly from the Bible. The title of the book, the appropriate chapter and verses are written down. Read the story by yourself, or with the help of parents or teachers. Use the MINI-DICTIONARY at the end of the book to help you find the meanings of the words in italics.

2nd   REFLECTION

Read the reflection, and as you do, think about the message contained in the story. What lessons can you learn from it?

3rd   PRAYERS

Say the prayer aloud or silently in your heart. You can also make up your own prayer.

4th   REVIEW

The REVIEW is designed to test how much you can remember of the stories you read.

5th   ARTWORK

Recall the story by using the frame provided to draw and color a picture for the story.

THE BOOKS OF THE NEW TESTAMENT

GOSPELS:
        MATTHEW
        MARK
        LUKE
        JOHN
HISTORY:
        THE ACTS OF THE APOSTLES
PAUL'S LETTERS:
        TO THE ROMANS
        FIRST LETTER TO THE CORINTHIANS
        SECOND LETTER TO THE CORINTHIANS
        TO THE GALATIANS
        TO THE EPHESIANS
        TO THE PHILIPPIANS
        TO THE COLOSSIANS
        FIRST LETTER TO THE THESSALONIANS
        SECOND LETTER TO THE THESSALONIANS
        FIRST LETTER TO TIMOTHY
        SECOND LETTER TO TIMOTHY
        TO TITUS
        TO PHILEMON
        TO THE HEBREWS
OTHER LETTERS:
        THE LETTER OF JAMES
        THE FIRST LETTER OF PETER
        THE SECOND LETTER OF PETER
        THE FIRST LETTER OF JOHN
        THE SECOND LETTER OF JOHN
        THE THIRD LETTER OF JOHN
        THE LETTER OF JUDE

        REVELATION

TABLE OF CONTENTS

TABLE OF CONTENTS

A VISIT FROM AN ANGEL
LUKE 1: 26-38

In the sixth month the angel Gabriel was sent by God to a town in Galilee called Nazareth, to a virgin engaged to a man whose name was Joseph, of the house of David. The virgin's name was Mary. And he came to her and said, "Greetings, *favored* one! The Lord is with you." But she was much perplexed by his words and pondered what sort of greeting this might be. The angel said to her, "Do not be afraid, Mary, for you have found favor with God. And now, you will *conceive* in your *womb* and bear a son, and you will name him Jesus. He will be great, and will be called the Son of the Most High, and the Lord God will give to him the throne of his *ancestor* David.

He will reign over the house of Jacob for ever, and of his kingdom there will be no end." Mary said to the angel, "How can this be, since I am a virgin?" The angel said to her, "The Holy Spirit will come upon you, and the power of the Most High will overshadow you; therefore the child to be born will be holy; he will be called Son of God. And now, your relative Elizabeth in her old age has also conceived a son; and this is the sixth month for her who was said to be barren. For nothing will be impossible with God." Then Mary said, "Here am I, the servant of the Lord; let it be done with me according to your word." Then the angel departed from her.

A VISIT FROM AN ANGEL

REFLECTION

Think about this! A long time ago God the Father made a promise to send a Savior to this earth. When the time was right, God kept His promise. Jesus came to live on earth. Mary his mother and Joseph his guardian welcomed him into their home and into their family. God kept His promise, are you careful to keep the promises you make? Children make promises too, like coming straight home from school, doing their homework regularly, cleaning their room, watching less television, and taking care of their clothes. Sometimes they break their promises. Children who break their promises can become unreliable and untrustworthy.

In this story we see that Mary was willing to do what God wanted her to do. Are you willing and ready to obey God, regardless of what He asks of you? Mary was a faithful and willing servant of God, and because of that she was rewarded greatly. She gave birth to God's Son, Jesus Christ.

PRAYER

Thank you Father God, you promised to send us a Savior, and you kept your promise. Help me to keep the promises I make. Thank you Mary, you listened to God's word, and accepted to bring Jesus into this world.

Amen.

A VISIT FROM AN ANGEL
REVIEW

CHOOSE THE RIGHT ANSWERS:

1. This story took place in a town called:
   A. Galilee
   B. Nazareth
   C. Jerusalem

2. Mary received a visit from:
   A. her mother
   B. her father
   C. an angel

3. The visitor's name was:
   A. Raphael
   B. Gabriel
   C. Michael

4. What did the visitor bring Mary?
   A. good news
   B. bad news
   C. gifts

5. Someone who is perplexed is:
   A. happy
   B. sad
   C. puzzled

A VISIT FROM AN ANGEL
ARTWORK

Use your imagination to create a picture for this story.

BORN IN BETHLEHEM
LUKE 2: 3-15

All went to their own towns to be *registered*. Joseph also went from the town of Nazareth in Galilee to Judea, to the city of David called Beth-le-hem, because he was descended from the house and family of David. He went to be registered with Mary, to whom he was engaged and who was expecting a child. While they were there, the time came for her to deliver her child. And she gave birth to her firstborn son and wrapped him in bands of cloth, and laid him in a *manger*, because there was no place for them in the inn.

In that region there were shepherds living in the fields, keeping watch over their flock by night. Then an angel of the Lord stood before them, and the glory of the Lord shone around them, and they were terrified. But the angel said to them, "Do not be afraid; for see - I am bringing you good news of great joy for all the people: to you is born this day in the city of David a Savior, who is the Messiah, the Lord. This will be a sign for you: you will find a child wrapped in bands of cloth and lying in a manger." And suddenly there was with the angel a multitude of the heavenly host, praising God and saying, "Glory to God in the highest heaven, and on earth peace among those whom he favors!" When the angels had left them and gone into heaven, the shepherds said to one another, "Let us go now to Beth-le-hem and see this thing that has taken place, which the Lord has made known to us."

BORN IN BETHLEHEM
REFLECTION

The birth of a baby can be a time of joy and happiness. Some parents proudly announce the news to their relatives and friends. So it was when the baby Jesus was born; an angel from heaven announced the good news to shepherds. The story said that the shepherds were terrified. Rightly so, can you imagine waking up in the middle of the night and seeing an angel standing before you? What would you do? Can you imagine how the shepherds felt when they saw a whole multitude of heavenly angels, and heard them singing a song of praise to God?

Now forget about how scared the shepherds were at seeing the angels, and think of a time in your life when you felt great excitement. Perhaps a new baby brother or sister was added to your family. Perhaps there was a wedding in your family, or perhaps it was your birthday celebration, or school graduation. Perhaps you were going on a family vacation to see the sights in another country. Certainly, you would feel great happiness! The shepherds too, must have felt great happiness as they proceeded on their way to Bethlehem to see the baby Jesus for themselves.

PRAYER

Jesus, you left heaven and came to earth because you loved us, and wanted to save us from our sins. Thank you for the joy and happiness you brought with you.

Amen

BORN IN BETHLEHEM
REVIEW

CHOOSE THE RIGHT ANSWER:

1. Where was Jesus born?
A. in Nazareth
B. in Galilee
C. in Bethlehem

2. Mary laid her baby in a:
A. palace
B. church
C. manger

3. As he lay in the manger, Jesus may have heard this sound.
A. woof-woof
B. meow
C. baa-baa

4. Jesus' first visitors were:
A. shepherds
B. a doctor
C. the inn keeper

5. Another word for terrified is:
A. fearful
B. sad
C. glad

BORN IN BETHLEHEM

ARTWORK

Use your imagination to create a picture for this story.

BOY JESUS IN THE TEMPLE
LUKE 2:41-52

Now every year his parents went to *Jerusalem* for the festival of the *Passover*. And when he was twelve years old, they went up as usual for the festival. When the festival was ended and they started to return, the boy Jesus stayed behind in Jerusalem, but his parents did not know it. Assuming that he was in the group of travelers, they went a day's journey. Then they started to look for him among their relatives and friends. When they did not find him, they returned to Jerusalem to search for him. After three days they found him in the temple, sitting among the teachers, listening to them and asking them questions. And all who heard him were amazed at his understanding and his answers. When his parents saw him they were astonished; and his mother said to him, "Child, why have you treated us like this? Look, your father and I have been searching for you in great anxiety." He said to them, "Why were you searching for me? Did you not know that I must be in my Father's house?" But they did not understand what he said to them. Then he went down with them and came to Nazareth, and was obedient to them. His mother treasured all these things in her heart. And Jesus increased in wisdom and in years, and in divine and human favor.

BOY JESUS IN THE TEMPLE
REFLECTION

Jesus showed us by his example that being in the temple was an important part of his life. There he found teachers. He listened to them, he questioned them, and he answered their questions. The story says that all who listened to him were amazed at his understanding and his answers. As a student, it is important to listen to your teachers carefully and to ask questions, whenever you hear something that you disagree with, or you do not clearly understand.

When his parents found him, Jesus went home with them and was obedient to them. Here Jesus is giving another good example, that of obedience to parents, and to those whom God has placed in authority over you. Jesus was glad to be in the temple, or as he called it, "My Father's House." Do you see your church as God's house? Do you go there regularly? When you go to church, are you happy to be there? Do you experience a sense of belonging in your Father's house? Do you do your part to make others feel joy and happiness there?

PRAYER

Jesus, thank you for the great examples you passed down to me. Help me to be a good student, and obey in all things that will help me to become a better child of God.

Amen

BOY JESUS IN THE TEMPLE
REVIEW

CHOOSE THE RIGHT ANSWER:

1. Jesus and his parents went to the Passover Festival:
A. every week
B. every month
C. every year

2. After the festival, who stayed behind in Jerusalem?
A. Joseph
B. Mary
C. Jesus

3. How old was the boy Jesus when he got lost?
A. 3 years
B. 12 years
C. 6 years

4. Jesus was found in his Father's:
A. store
B. house
C. car

5. Someone who is obedient is willing to submit to:
A. scores
B. records
C. authority

BOY JESUS IN THE TEMPLE
ARTWORK

Use your imagination to create a picture for this story.

JESUS IS TEMPTED
LUKE 4:1-13

Jesus, full of the Holy Spirit, returned from the *Jordan* and was led by the Spirit in the wilderness, where for forty days he was tempted by the devil. He ate nothing at all during those days, and when they were over, he was famished. The devil said to him, "If you are the Son of God, command this stone to become a loaf of bread." Jesus answered him, "It is written, 'One does not live by bread alone.'"

Then the devil led him up and showed him in an instant all the kingdoms of the world. And the devil said to him, "To you I will give their glory and all this authority; for it has been given over to me, and I give it to anyone I please. If you, then, will worship me, it will all be yours." Jesus answered him, "It is written, 'Worship the Lord your God, and serve only him.'" Then the devil took him to Jerusalem, and placed him on the *pinnacle* of the *temple*, saying to him, "If you are the Son of God, throw yourself down from here, for it is written, 'He will command his angels concerning you to protect you,' and 'On their hands they will bear you up, so that you will not dash your foot against a stone.'" Jesus answered him, "It is said, 'Do not put the Lord your God to the test.'" When the devil had finished every test, he departed from him until an opportune time.

JESUS IS TEMPTED
REFLECTION

After Jesus had fasted for forty days he was very hungry. Satan appeared to him and tempted him to satisfy his hunger by making bread from a stone, but Jesus rebuked him, and refused to obey his command. Satan returned with a second temptation. This time the devil used money, riches and wealth, to lure Jesus into idolatry, but Jesus was not amused. He said what is important is to worship God and serve Him only. Thirdly, Satan wanted Jesus to show off his strength, his power, his glory, and his divinity by throwing himself down from the top of the temple, but Jesus refused to obey.

Notice that Satan quoted Scripture verses to Jesus in an attempt to influence him to do wrong. Jesus responded by quoted Scripture verses, too. You too will face many temptations every day. Some of these temptations will sound so convincing that you will want to give in to them, but you can call on your friend Jesus to help you resist the temptations that you know are wrong.

PRAYER

Lord Jesus, temptations keep coming my way every day, but when I read about how you dealt with your temptations, it gives me the courage to face my temptations boldly, and I know that I will be victorious.

Amen

JESUS IS TEMPTED
REVIEW

CHOOSE THE RIGHT ANSWER:

1.   This story took place in the:
A.   church
B.   park
C.   wilderness

2.   Another word for wilderness is:
A.   waste land
B.   city
C.   country

3.   This encounter took place between Jesus and the:
A.   devil
B.   people
C.   disciples

4.   An opportune time is a:
A.   suitable time
B.   a great time
C.   a solemn time

5.   To eat nothing at all is to:
A.   fast
B.   drink
C.   cook

JESUS IS TEMPTED

ARTWORK

Use your imagination to create a picture for this story.

FOLLOW ME
MARK 1:14-20

Now after John was arrested, Jesus came to Galilee, proclaiming the good news of God, and saying, "The time is fulfilled, and the kingdom of God has come near; repent, and believe in the good news."

As Jesus passed along the Sea of Galilee, he saw Simon and his brother Andrew casting a net into the sea - for they were fishermen. And Jesus said to them, "Follow me and I will make you fish for people." And immediately they left their nets and followed him. As he went a little farther, he saw James son of Zeb.e.dee and his brother John, who were in their boat mending the nets. Immediately he called them; and they left their father Zeb.e.dee in the boat with the *hired men*, and followed him.

FOLLOW ME

REFLECTION

Jesus called Simon Peter, Andrew, James and John to follow him and proclaim the good news of God. Jesus is calling you too, to tell others about God. Would you be willing to dedicate your life to learning and teaching the Word of God? This is a great challenge, because there are many temptations in today's world that make it difficult to live righteously and to follow Jesus' example. You can learn about Jesus' teachings by listening attentively to your teachers in the Religious Education classes, you can read the Bible for yourself, and ask questions about what you read. You can join discussion groups, and exchange ideas. These are wonderful ways to help you grow in your knowledge of God's Word, and make it known to others who are hungry to hear it!

The disciples must have felt honored and welcomed because Jesus called them to follow him. Have you ever called and welcomed children who would like to play in your group? If you did, you have done a good job of spreading the God- kind of love. You have also made your contribution to making the world a better place.

PRAYER

Dear Jesus, I want to know more about you. I want to follow your teaching. Give me the grace to listen attentively to my parents, teachers, and others who impart your Word to me. In turn, I will do my best to help others follow in your footsteps.

Amen

FOLLOW ME

REVIEW

CHOOSE THE RIGHT ANSWER:

1. Jesus passed along the Sea of:
A. Tiberius
B. Jordan
C. Galilee

2. The first two disciples chosen were James and John.
A. true
B. false
C. I do not know

3. Who said, "Follow me and I will make you fish for people?"
A. Peter
B. James
C. Jesus

4. When did Simon and Andrew respond to Jesus' call?
A. the next day
B. immediately
C. later

5. Someone who is a fisherman catches:
A. fish
B. insects
C. people

FOLLOW ME

ARTWORK

Use your imagination to create a picture for this story.

CANA OF GALILEE
John 2:1-11

On the third day there was a wedding in Cana of *Galilee*, and the mother of Jesus was there. Jesus and his disciples had also been invited to the wedding. When the wine gave out, the mother of Jesus said to him, "They have no wine." And Jesus said to her, "Woman, what concern is that to you and me? My hour has not yet come." His mother said to the servants, "Do whatever he tells you." Now standing there were six stone water jars for the Jewish rites of purification, each holding twenty or thirty gallons. Jesus said to them, "Fill the jars with water." And they filled them up to the brim. He said to them, "Now draw some out, and take it to the chief *steward*." So they took it. When the steward tasted the water that had become wine, and did not know where it came from (though the servants who had drawn the water knew), the steward called the bridegroom and said to him, "Everyone serves the good wine first, and then the *inferior wine* after the guests have become drunk. But you have kept the good wine until now." Jesus did this, the first of his signs, in Cana of Galilee, and revealed his glory; and his disciples believed in him.

CANA OF GALILEE

REFLECTION

Think of a celebration as a time for joy, happiness, reunions, dancing, delicious foods, and drink! In this story Jesus was invited to a wedding celebration. His mother and his disciples were there, too. Everyone was having a good time, and before the celebration was over, all of the wine was already consumed.

Jesus' mother, Mary, must have been keeping a close watch over the situation, because it was she who noticed that all of the wine was gone. No doubt, this was an embarrassing situation for the bridegroom. Mary showed her trust in Jesus by taking the problem to him. She believed in his ability to answer prayers, and even though his 'hour had not yet come,' he granted her request.

In this story Mary sets a good example for us by trusting in Jesus and asking him for help, and Jesus sets a good example for us by obeying his mother and granting her request. Are you confident enough to trust Jesus like Mary did?

PRAYER

Lord Jesus, grant me the grace to be as observant as your mother Mary was, so that I can help others who are in need.

Amen

CANA OF GALILEE

REVIEW

CHOOSE THE RIGHT ANSWER:

1. Who or what is Cana?
A. an animal
B. a place
C. a thing

2. Cana is a story about:
A. a party
B. a picnic
C. a wedding

3. Jesus, his mother and his disciples were present at the wedding.
A. true
B. false
C. I am not sure

4. When the wine gave out Mary took the problem to:
A. Jesus
B. Joseph
C. an angel

5. Someone who is invited is specially:
A. turned away
B. scolded
C. called

CANA OF GALILEE

ARTWORK

Use your imagination to create a picture for this story.

JESUS AND ZACCHAEUS
LUKE 19:1-10

Jesus entered Jericho and was passing through it. A man was there named Zac.chae.us; he was a chief tax collector and was rich. He was trying to see who Jesus was, but on account of the crowd he could not, because he was short in *stature*. So he ran ahead and climbed a sycamore tree to see him, because he was going to pass that way. When Jesus came to the place, he looked up and said to him, "Zac.chae.us, hurry and come down; for I must stay at your house today." So he hurried down and was happy to welcome him. All who saw it began to grumble and said, "He has gone to be the guest of one who is a sinner." Zac. chae.us stood there and said to the Lord, "Look, half of my possessions, Lord, I will give to the poor; and if I have defrauded anyone of anything, I will pay back four times as much." Then Jesus said to him, "Today salvation has come to this house, because he too is a son of *Abraham*. For the Son of Man came to seek out and to save the lost."

JESUS AND ZACCHAEUS

REFLECTION

Like Zacchaeus, sometimes we too, do things that we are not pleased about. Sometimes we would like to correct our mistakes, but we find it hard to make things right. Fortunately for us, God is willing to forgive our mistakes, and forget about them. To show how truly sorry Zacchaeus was for his mistakes, he was willing to do whatever it took to make things right with God and with his neighbors.

Some children often do wrong by teasing, rejecting, or bullying other children. If you have done any of these things, or anything else that you know is wrong, ask for forgiveness; forgiveness from God and from the one you hurt. Like Zacchaeus, show God that you are willing to change your heart and do what is right. Also, if others have wronged you, be willing to forgive them, so that God can forgive the wrongs you have done.

PRAYER

Jesus, I am sorry for engaging in wrong doing. Please forgive me, just as I am ready to forgive others who have done wrong things to me.

Amen

JESUS AND ZACCHAEUS
REVIEW

CHOOSE THE RIGHT ANSWER:

1. Jesus was passing through:
A. Jericho
B. Jerusalem
C. Joppa

2. Zacchaeus wanted to see:
A. the disciples
B. Jesus
C. Mary

3. In order to see Jesus, Zacchaeus ran ahead and climbed a:
A. fence
B. tree
C. ladder

4. After Zacchaeus met Jesus, he changed his:
A. money
B. house
C. lifestyle

5. Another word for defrauded is:
A. cheated
B. robbed
C. all of the above

JESUS AND ZACCHAEUS
ARTWORK

Use your imagination to create a picture for this story.

IS THIS THE CHRIST?
JOHN 7:25-31

Now some of the people of Jerusalem were saying, "Is not this the man whom they are trying to kill? And here he is, speaking openly, but they say nothing to him! Can it be that the authorities really know that this is the *Messiah*? Yet we know where this man is from; but when the Messiah comes, no one will know where he is from." Then Jesus cried out as he was teaching in the temple, "You know me, and you know where I am from. I have not come on my own. But the one who sent me is true, and you do not know him. I know him, because I am from him, and he sent me." Then they tried to arrest him, but no one laid hands on him, because his hour had not yet come. Yet many in the crowd believed in him and were saying, "When the Messiah comes, will he do more signs than this man has done?"

IS THIS THE CHRIST?

REFLECTION

The people were having a hard time trying to figure out who Jesus really was. Was he the Christ? Was he the Savior they were expecting? How is it that some people were trying to kill him? It is because he spoke out against some of their customs and traditions? Others believed his message, and yet others were not sure what to think and what to believe.

Do you also wonder in your mind about who Jesus is? Is he the person he said he is? Is he really the Son of God? Can he really do the things he said he could do? Is he truly the Messiah? Did he really come to redeem us from sin? When these questions arise in your mind, go to the Bible for answers. There are many Bibles written just for children. You can ask your parents and teachers to help you find answers to your questions. Jesus wants you to know him, love him, and serve him in this world, and be happy with him in heaven. So to fulfill your goal of knowing all you can about Jesus, spend time learning about him by studying God's word in your Bible.

PRAYER

Dear Jesus, help me to know you more, love you more, and serve you more as I go about my daily duty.

Amen

IS THIS THE CHRIST?

REVIEW

CHOOSE THE RIGHT ANSWER:

1. This story took place in:
A. Nazareth
B. Jerusalem
C. Bethlehem

2. According to the story, Jesus was teaching in the:
A. church
B. temple
C. marketplace

3. The authorities did not arrest Jesus, because it was not his:
A. hour
B. day
C. season

4. Some believed in Jesus because they witnessed his:
A. accident
B. signs
C. baptism

5. Someone who is speaking openly is talking:
A. nonsense
B. freely
C. loudly

IS THIS THE CHRIST?

ARTWORK

Use your imagination to create a picture for this story.

JESUS FEEDS THE CROWD
MARK 6:34-44

As he went ashore, he saw a great crowd; and he had compassion for them, because they were like sheep without a shepherd; and he began to teach them many things. When it grew late his disciples came to him and said, "This is a deserted place, and the hour is now very late; send them away so that they may go into the surrounding country and villages and buy something for themselves to eat." But he answered them, "You give them something to eat." They said to him, "Are we to go and buy two hundred *denarii* worth of bread, and give it to them to eat?" And he said to them," How many loaves have you? Go and see." When they had found out, they said, "Five, and two fish." Then he ordered them to get all the people to sit down in groups on the green grass. So they sat down in groups of hundreds and of fifties. Taking the five loaves and the two fish, he looked up to heaven, and blessed and broke the loaves, and gave them to the disciples to set before the people; and he divided the two fish among them all. And all ate and were filled; and they took up twelve baskets full of broken pieces and of the fish. Those who had eaten the loaves numbered five thousand men.

JESUS FEEDS THE CROWD

REFLECTION

Reflect on what happened at Cana. Jesus solved the problem of the lack of wine, by providing more wine. Now in this story, we read how Jesus solved the lack of food by providing more food. Thousands of people came to see Jesus and to listen to him. They were so engrossed in his teaching, that they did not realize how late it was, until it was too late for them to go out and buy food for themselves. The disciples became concerned and like Mary at Cana, they reached out to Jesus for help.

In this story, Jesus took what they had—five loaves and two fish and miraculously changed them into more than enough for everyone. This story teaches us to trust Jesus and not to worry about whether or not he will provide for us. He will always provide for us. However, it is not enough to simply ask for what we need and then sit back and wait for it to come. Jesus is not inviting us to be lazy, nor will Jesus provide for us magically. No! Just like the disciples had to follow Jesus' instructions, so we too, must do our part; we must follow Jesus' instructions to obtain what we need.

PRAYER

Jesus, there are many children in the world who do not have enough to eat. Help me to remember this, and do my share to help the poor and needy.

Amen

JESUS FEEDS THE CROWD
REVIEW

CHOOSE THE RIGHT ANSWER:

1. This story took place in a deserted:
A. basement
B. field
C. place

2. Who were told to give the people something to eat?
A. Jesus
B. disciples
C. cooks

3. To be a disciple is to follow a:
A. joker
B. leader
C. stranger

4. How many baskets of broken pieces were taken up?
A. twelve
B. six
C. five

5. Someone who is following on foot is:
A. walking
B. on a camel
C. on a donkey

JESUS FEEDS THE CROWD
ARTWORK

Use your imagination to create a picture for this story.

JESUS HEALS BARTIMAEUS
MARK 10:46-52

They came to Jericho. As he and his disciples and a large crowd were leaving Jericho, Bartimaeus son of Timaeus, a blind beggar, was sitting by the roadside. When he heard that it was Jesus of Nazareth, he began to shout out and say, "Jesus, Son of David, have mercy on me!" Many *sternly* ordered him to be quiet, but he cried out even more loudly, "Son of David, have mercy on me!" Jesus stood still and said, "Call him here." And they called the blind man, saying to him, "Take heart; get up, he is calling you." So throwing off his cloak, he sprang up and came to Jesus. Then Jesus said to him, "What do you want me to do for you?" The blind man said to him, "My teacher, let me see again." Jesus said to him, "Go; your faith has made you well." Immediately he regained his sight and followed him on the way.

JESUS HEALS BARTIMAEUS

REFLECTION

Although many people wanted Bartimaeus to keep quiet, he persisted in begging Jesus to heal him. Jesus rewarded him by giving him back his sight. Bartimaeus received his sight because he had the faith to believe that Jesus could do it.

Bartimaeus could not see, because he was blind. Even though you and I can see, sometimes we can be blind in different ways. We can be blind to the poor who need our help. We can be blind to our friends who need our help. We can be blind to family members who ask us to help with chores around the house. Maintaining awareness and thinking of others can make us better persons.

PRAYER

Dear God, I thank you for the wonderful gift of sight. I want to become more aware of others who need my help, and do what I can to help them.

Amen

JESUS HEALS BARTIMAEUS
REVIEW

CHOOSE THE RIGHT ANSWER:

1. What did Bartimaeus do when he was ordered to be quiet?
A. cried even louder
B. pouted
C. shouted out

2. How did Bartimaeus know Jesus was passing by?
A. he heard
B. he saw
C. he touched

3. Who shouted, "Jesus, son of David, have mercy on me!"
A. Timaeus
B. the people
C. Bartimaeus

4. What did Jesus give Bartimaeus?
A. taste
B. sight
C. hearing

5. Another word for regained is:
A. got back
B. replayed
C. none of the above

JESUS HEALS BARTIMAEUS

ARTWORK

Use your imagination to create a picture for this story.

THE GOOD SHEPHERD
JOHN 10: 11-21

"I am the good shepherd. The good shepherd lays down his life for the sheep. The hired hand, who is not the shepherd and does not own the sheep sees the wolf coming and leaves the sheep and runs away - and the wolf snatches them and scatters them. The hired hand runs away because a hired hand does not care for the sheep. I am the good shepherd. I know my own and my own know me, just as the Father knows me and I know the Father. And I lay down my life for the sheep. I have other sheep that do not belong to this fold. I must bring them also, and they will listen to my voice. So there will be one flock, one shepherd. For this reason the Father loves me, because I lay down my life in order to take it up again. No one takes it from me, but I lay it down of my own *accord*. I have power to lay it down, and I have power to take it up again. I have received this command from my Father." Again the Jews were divided because of these words. Many of them were saying, "He has a demon and is out of his mind. Why listen to him?" Others were saying, "These are not the words of one who has a demon. Can a demon open the eyes of the blind?"

THE GOOD SHEPHERD

REFLECTION

Jesus calls himself the Good Shepherd. The good shepherd takes good care of his sheep, making sure that they have all their needs satisfied. If necessary, the good shepherd might even die to save his sheep. In this story Jesus is our shepherd and we are his sheep. He died for us to show how much he loves us.

Are you good to one another? Can you say that you are a good friend to your classmates, a good student to your teachers or a good child to your parents? Some of the people mistook Jesus' goodness for madness. They said that he had a demon and was out of his mind. However, some had faith in Jesus. They recognized that his words were those of true righteousness, and his acts were those of divinity. Jesus' teachings may be difficult for us to understand, and his actions may be difficult for us to believe, but as believers we believe that Christ is our true shepherd, and he takes good care of us.

PRAYERS

Dear Jesus, I pray that one day, all Christians and non-Christians alike, will be brought together into one fold with you as their one shepherd.

Amen

THE GOOD SHEPHERD
REVIEW

CHOOSE THE RIGHT ANSWER:

1. What does the good shepherd lay down for his sheep?
A. blanket
B. grain
C. life

2. Another word for hired hand is:
A. farmer
B. paid worker
C. priest

3. Who leaves the sheep and runs away?
A. the hired hand
B. the mother
C. the Dad

4. Who or what snatches and scatters the sheep?
A. a donkey
B. a shepherd
C. a wolf

5. To bring into one fold is to take into the:
A. water
B. group
C. forest

THE CHILDREN'S FRIEND

ARTWORK

Use your imagination to create a picture for this story.

THE CHILDREN'S FRIEND
MARK 10:13-16; MATTHEW 18:1-5; 10

People were bringing little children to him in order that he might touch them; and the disciples spoke sternly to them. But when Jesus saw this, he was *indignant* and said to them, "Let the little children come to me; do not stop them; for it is to such as these that the kingdom of God belongs. Truly I tell you, whoever does not receive the kingdom of God as a little child will never enter it." And he took them up in his arms, laid his hands on them, and blessed them.

At that time the disciples came to Jesus and asked, "Who is the greatest in the kingdom of heaven?" He called a child, whom he put among them, and said, "Truly I tell you, unless you change and become like children, you will never enter the kingdom of heaven. Whoever becomes humble like this child is the greatest in the kingdom of heaven. Whoever welcomes one such child in my name welcomes me. Take care that you do not *despise* one of these little ones; for, I tell you, in heaven their angels continually see the face of my Father in heaven."

THE CHILDREN'S FRIEND

REFLECTION

By rebuking the disciples for speaking harshly to the people, Jesus showed how much he cared for little children. He cared so much for them that he took time off from his busy schedule to spend a few precious moments with them. Yes, Jesus has great love and consideration for children. I can imagine hearing him asking the children where they were going, or what they would like him to do for them. Perhaps some of them must have climbed on his lap, and questioned him too. Then Jesus blessed them.

Jesus has the same love and consideration for today's children. Grown-ups have to be careful how they treat God's little ones, because they have angels who are always talking to God about the little ones they are protecting here on earth. Everyone who wishes to enter the kingdom of heaven will do well to adopt some childlike qualities like humility, trust, simplicity, obedience, politeness, faith, meekness, and a willingness to be taught the truths about God's Kingdom.

PRAYER

Thank you Jesus, you do love little children. We love you, too. Help us to show that same love to others.

Amen

THE CHILDREN'S FRIEND
REVIEW

CHOOSE THE RIGHT ANSWER:

1. What did the people want Jesus to do for the children?
A. feed them
B. touch them
C. anoint them

2. The disciples spoke kindly to the people.
A. true
B. false
C. I am not sure

3. How do you suppose the people felt about the disciples' action?
A. disappointed
B. pleased
C. happy

4. How do you suppose the children felt after they were blessed?
A. unhappy
B. loved
C. disappointed

5. What is the opposite of humble?
A. sad
B. proud
C. busy

THE CHILDREN'S FRIEND
ARTWORK

Use your imagination to create a picture for this story.

JESUS WALKS ON WATER
MATTHEW 14:22-32

Immediately he made the disciples get into the boat and go on ahead to the other side, while he dismissed the crowds. And after he had dismissed the crowds, he went up the mountain by himself to pray. When evening came, he was there alone, but by this time the boat, *battered* by the waves, was far from the land, for the wind was against them. And early in the morning he came walking towards them on the sea. But when the disciples saw him walking on the sea, they were terrified, saying, "It is a ghost!" And they cried out in fear. But immediately Jesus spoke to them and said, "Take heart, it is I; do not be afraid." Peter answered him, "Lord, if it is you, command me to come to you on the water." He said, "Come." So Peter got out of the boat, started walking on the water, and came toward Jesus. But when he noticed the strong wind, he became frightened, and beginning to sink, he cried out, "Lord, save me!" Jesus immediately reached out his hand and caught him, "You of little faith, why did you doubt?" When they got back into the boat the wind ceased. And those in the boat worshipped him, saying, "Truly you are the Son of God."

JESUS WALKS ON WATER

REFLECTION

In this story, as the disciples were struggling against a natural disaster of waves, and wind, Jesus showed up. How did the disciples react? They were terrified! They did not recognize their teacher. They turned to fear and doubt. Peter was the only one brave enough to get out of the boat and walk on the water. However, brave Peter, as he started walking on the water took his eyes off Jesus, and looked at the strong wind. He became frightened, and began to sink. Instantly, he knew who to call on for help, and he cried out, "Lord, save me!" Jesus restored his faith and they walked back to the boat together.

These disciples, particularly Peter, had a relationship with Jesus and so do you. Jesus is very close to you. Are you able to make time during the day to pray? Occasionally, Jesus took time-out, and climbed up a mountain to be alone with God and pray. You do not have to climb up a mountain to pray; you can make your own mountain in your mind and spend a few minutes a day in prayer with your God. Do not let fear, doubt, disbelief, anxieties, worry, or frustration draw you away from God.

PRAYER

Dear Jesus, I believe in you. I trust you. I love you. Help me to cast fear and doubt out of my mind, and continue strong in my faith in you.

Amen

JESUS WALKS ON WATER
REVIEW

CHOOSE THE RIGHT ANSWER:

1. Who dismissed the crowds?
A. Peter
B. Jesus
C. John

2. Jesus went up the mountain to:
A. pray
B. fast
C. eat

3. Early in the morning, Jesus came walking on:
A. a cloud
B. the sea
C. a boat

4. The apostles mistook Jesus for a:
A. cloud
B. ghost
C. wave

5. Someone who is frightened is:
A. lost
B. scared
C. annoyed

JESUS WALKS ON WATER
ARTWORK

Use your imagination to create a picture for this story.

JESUS IS REJECTED
LUKE 4:16-20; 24 -26, 28-30

When he came to Nazareth, where he had been brought up, he went to the synagogue on the Sabbath day, as was his custom. He stood up to read, and the scroll of the prophet, I.sai.ah was given to him. He unrolled the scroll and found the place where it was written: "The Spirit of the Lord is upon me, because he has anointed me to bring good news to the poor. He has sent me to proclaim release to the captives and recovery of sight to the blind, to let the oppressed go free, to proclaim the year of the Lord's favor." And he rolled up the scroll, gave it back to the attendant, and sat down.

And he said, "Truly I tell you, no prophet is accepted in the prophet's hometown. But the truth is, there were many widows in Israel in the time of Elijah, when the heaven was shut up three years and six months, and there was a severe famine over all the land; yet Elijah was sent to none of them except to a widow at Zar.e.phath in Sidon.

When they heard this, all in the synagogue were filled with rage. They got up, drove him out of the town, and led him to the brow of the hill on which their town was built, so that they might hurl him off the cliff. But he passed through the midst of them and went on his way.

JESUS IS REJECTED

REFLECTION

When Jesus returned to his hometown, he went to church. Luke makes a point of recording this. For Jesus, this was his custom, meaning he did it all the time. I think that Jesus found great delight in going to the synagogue, which is church as we know it today. He did not simply sit in church waiting for the service to end. No, Jesus participated. He took the scroll and read from it. All of the people knew Jesus. He grew up in their town, and as a child he must have played with them, yet when he said something they did not want to hear, they rejected him and tried to push him off a cliff.

Do you sometimes feel rejected, too? Do your classmates push you aside, call you names, laugh at you, and make fun of you? Do they decide not to choose you for a game? Do you feel rejected because you are different? You are not alone. Jesus was rejected too, so when you feel rejected, call on your friend, Jesus. Remember if Jesus was rejected, you will be rejected, too, but be brave. Jesus is with you. You can tell him all about it.

PRAYER

Jesus, grant me the courage to persevere when others reject me. Help me to think kindly of others, even when they treat me unfairly.

Amen

JESUS IS REJECTED

REVIEW

CHOOSE THE RIGHT ANSWER:

1. Was Jesus born in Nazareth?
A. yes
B. no
C. I do not know

2. Jesus was born in:
A. Galilee
B. Bethlehem
C. Jerusalem

3. On the Sabbath Day Jesus went to the:
A. synagogue
B. arena
C. library

4. From which book of the Bible did Jesus read?
A. Luke
B. Psalms
C. Isaiah

5. Someone who is oppressed is:
A. free
B. strange
C. persecuted

JESUS IS REJECTED

ARTWORK

Use your imagination to create a picture for this story.

A GIRL IS RESTORED TO LIFE
MARK 5: 22-24, 35-42

Then one of the leaders of the synagogue named Ja-i-rus came and, when he saw him, fell at his feet and begged him repeatedly, "My little daughter is at the point of death. Come and lay your hands on her, so that she may be made well, and live." So he went with him. Some people came from the leader's house to say, "Your daughter is dead. Why trouble the teacher any further?" But overhearing what they said, Jesus said to the leader of the synagogue, "Do not fear, only believe." He allowed no one to follow him except Peter, James and John, the brother of James. When they came to the house of the leader of the synagogue, he saw a commotion, people weeping and wailing loudly. When he had entered he said to them, "Why do you make a commotion and weep?" The child is not dead but sleeping." And they laughed at him. Then he put them all outside, and took the child's father and mother and those who were with him, and went in where the child was. He took her by the hand and said to her, "Tal-i-tha-cum," which means, "Little girl, get up!" And immediately the girl got up and began to walk about (she was twelve years of age).

A GIRL IS RESTORED TO LIFE

REFLECTION

The people in this story can be divided into two groups.

1. Those who believed in Jesus.
2. Those who did not believe in Jesus.

When Jesus said that the child was not dead, but sleeping, the disbelievers laughed at him. Jesus took the believers into the child's room and worked a miracle. He raised the dead girl to life. The believers witnessed the miracle, while the disbelievers were left outside.

On which side are you? Are you with the believers or the disbelievers? Those who believe will continue to experience signs and wonders from Jesus. Jesus rewards those who believe in him. He opened the eyes of the blind, he opened the ears of the deaf, he made the lame walk, and he raised some people from the dead, like the little girl in this story. Stories like this one can cause your faith in Jesus to grow. Remain on the side of the believers.

PRAYERS

Dear Jesus, I believe in you and what your word teaches. Help me to continue strong in my faith.

Amen

A GIRL IS RESTORED TO LIFE
REVIEW

CHOOSE THE RIGHT ANSWER:

1. The little girl's father was one of the leaders of:
A. the band
B. the synagogue
C. the army

2. The little girl was not with her father, because she was:
A. in school
B. very sick
C. with a friend

3. What did Jairus want Jesus to do for him?
A. give him bread
B. heal him
C. heal his daughter

4. Was Jairus' prayer answered?
A. yes
B. no
C. none of the above

5. Someone who is wailing is:
A. crying loudly
B. laughing
C. smiling

A GIRL IS RESTORED TO LIFE
ARTWORK

Use your imagination to create a picture for this story.

THE RICH YOUNG MAN
MATTHEW 19:16-23, 25-26

Then someone came to him and said, "Teacher, what good deed must I do to have eternal life?" and he said to him, "Why do you ask me about what is good? There is only one who is good. If you wish to enter into life, keep the commandments." He said to him, "Which ones?" and Jesus said, "You shall not murder; You shall not commit adultery; You shall not steal; You shall not bear false witness; Honor your father and your mother; also, You shall love your neighbor as yourself." The young man said to him, "I have kept all these; what do I still lack?" Jesus said to him, "If you wish to be perfect, go, sell your possessions, and give the money to the poor, and you will have treasure in heaven; then come, follow me." When the young man heard this word, he went away grieving, for he had many possessions. Then Jesus said to his disciples, "Truly I tell you, it will be hard for a rich man to enter the kingdom of heaven." When the disciples heard this, they were greatly astounded and said, "Then who can be saved?" But Jesus looked at them and said, "For mortals it is impossible, but for God all things are possible."

THE RICH YOUNG MAN
REFLECTION

The rich young man boasted that he kept all of the commandments. Since he was so good and holy, Jesus loved him and wanted him to be a follower, but on one condition. He had to sell all of his possessions and give the money to the poor. Selling his stuff was too painful, so he walked away grieving. His possessions had taken the place of God in his life.

Do you have things that are more precious to you than God? How about your card collection, your toy car collection, your computer games, your clothes? No one is telling you to sell everything and give the money to the poor, but you should be happy to make time during each day to strengthen your friendship with God. As for the poor, remember that they are in your midst, and whatever you can do to make their lives a little better, do so without grieving.

PRAYER

Dear God, grant me wisdom, so that I will always be able to make wise choices in all that I do and say.

Amen

THE RICH YOUNG MAN
REVIEW

CHOOSE THE RIGHT ANSWER:

1. In this story, who is referred to as Teacher?
A. Jesus
B. someone
C. the rich young man

2. How many commandments did the rich young man keep?
A. six
B. a few
C. all

3. Was the rich young man ready to give up his possessions?
A. yes
B. no
C. perhaps

4. Someone who is grieving is full of:
A. sorrow
B. humor
C. laughter

5. Mortals refer to:
A. persons
B. plants
C. spirits

THE RICH YOUNG MAN

ARTWORK

Use your imagination to create a picture for this story.

LABORERS IN THE VINEYARD
MATTHEW 20:1-12

The kingdom of heaven is like a landowner who went out early in the morning to hire laborers for his vineyard. After agreeing with the laborers for the usual daily wage, he sent them into his vineyard. When he went out about nine o'clock, he saw others standing idle in the marketplace; and he said to them, 'You also go into the vineyard and I will pay you what is right.' So they went. When he went out again about noon and about three o'clock, he did the same. And about five o'clock, he went out and found others standing around; and he said to them, 'Why are you standing here idle all day?' They said to him, 'Because no one has hired us.'

He said to them, 'You also go into the vineyard.' When evening came, the owner of the vineyard said to his manager, 'Call the laborers and give them their pay, beginning with the last and then going to the first.' When those hired about five o'clock came, each of them received the usual daily wage. Now when the first came, they thought they would receive more; but each of them also received the usual daily wage. And when they received it, they grumbled against the landowner, saying, 'These last worked only one hour and you have made them equal to us who have borne the burden of the day and the scorching heat.'

LABORERS IN THE VINEYARD

REFLECTION

The kingdom of God is open to all of us. We are all God's children. He calls us all to be happy in His kingdom. We have Jesus' word for it. Jesus once said that in his Father's house there are many dwelling places, and he was going to prepare a place for us. (John 14:2-3) There is a place for each of us in God's kingdom. Our place will be there, but God will not force His kingdom on any of us.

In this story, the laborers were not all sent into the vineyard at the same time. So it is with us, we will not all accept the word of God at the same time. Some of us will accept early in life, others will accept later in life, others will accept in their old age and others on their deathbed. At whatever time we accept the kingdom, we will all be welcomed in the same way. There is no need to be jealous or envious if we see others accepting the word of God ahead of us. Simply thank God for them and remember our time will come too.

PRAYER

Jesus, help us to realize that when our work on this earth is finished, you will be waiting to receive us in your kingdom.

Amen

LABORERS IN THE VINEYARD
REVIEW

CHOOSE THE RIGHT ANSWER:

1. Jesus compares the Kingdom of God to a:
A. jeweler
B. farmer
C. landowner

2. The landowner's business was:
A. grapes
B. tomatoes
C. cherries

3. In this story who do you think the landowner represents?
A. man
B. angel
C. God

4. How would you describe this landowner?
A. unfair
B. generous
C. selfish

5. Someone who is generous gives:
A. freely
B. sparingly
C. grudgingly

LABORERS IN THE VINEYARD

ARTWORK

Use your imagination to create a picture for this story.

NICODEMUS VISITS JESUS
JOHN 3:1-10

Now there was a *Phar.i.
see* named Nic.o.de.mus, a
leader of the Jews. He came
to Jesus by night and said
to him, "*Rabbi*, we know that
you are a teacher who has
come from God; for no one
can do these signs that you
do apart from the presence
of God." Jesus answered him,
"Very truly, I tell you, no
one can see the kingdom of
God without being born from
above." Nic.o.de.mus said to
Jesus, "How can anyone be
born after having grown old?
Can one enter a second time
into the mother's womb and
be born?" Jesus answered,
"Very truly, I tell you, no one
can enter the kingdom of God
without being born of water
and Spirit. What is born of
the flesh is flesh, and what
is born of the Spirit is spirit.
Do not be astonished that I
said to you, 'You must be born
from above.' The wind blows
where it chooses, and you
hear the sound of it, but you
do not know where it comes
from or where it goes. So it
is with everyone who is born
of the Spirit." Nic.o.de.mus
said to him, "How can these
things be?" Jesus answered
him, "Are you a teacher of
Israel, and yet you do not
understand these things?"

NICODEMUS VISITS JESUS

REFLECTION

Here is someone who had questions that he could not answer, and he felt that the only person who could enlighten him was Jesus, so he went to Jesus at night. Why by night? Perhaps, he was afraid that his peers would find out that he was keeping company with Jesus and mock him for doing so.

Sometimes we feel like Nicodemus. We feel that if we go to church, others will mock us; if we do acts of kindness, others will mock us, if we read our Bible, others will mock us. Like Nicodemus, we have to seek out a way to continue to keep company with Jesus so we can do things his way. His way is the right way. In following Jesus we too will have questions. We ask them, but sometimes we do not get the answers that satisfy us. We become puzzled and so we have to ask other questions. If we do not give up our quest for the answers, we will get them. Like Nicodemus, we must seek out the right persons who will show patience, understanding, and knowledge in listening to us and answering our questions.

PRAYER

Jesus, send us teachers who can teach us about you, and grant us the grace to understand what we hear.

Amen

NICODEMUS VISITS JESUS

REVIEW

CHOOSE THE RIGHT ANSWER:

1. Who visited Jesus at night?
A. Bartimaeus
B. Nicodemus
C. Zacchaeus

2. Nicodemus visited Jesus because he wanted some:
A. bread
B. books
C. answers

3. No one can enter the kingdom without being born of:
A. water
B. Spirit
C. both

4. Nicodemus was a:
A. leader of the Jews
B. teacher of Israel
C. both

5. Someone who is astonished is:
A. guilty
B. amazed
C. condemned

NICODEMUS VISITS JESUS

ARTWORK

Use your imagination to create a picture for this story.

JESUS HEALS A WOMAN
LUKE 13: 10-17

Now he was teaching in one of the synagogues on the Sabbath. And just then there appeared a woman with a spirit that had crippled her for eighteen years. She was bent over and was quite unable to stand up straight. When Jesus saw her, he called her over and said, "Woman, you are set free from your *ailment.*" When he laid his hands on her, immediately she stood up straight and began praising God. But the leader of the synagogue, indignant that Jesus had cured on the Sabbath, kept saying to the crowd, "There are six days on which work ought to be done; come on those days and be cured, and not on the Sabbath day." But the Lord answered him and said, "You *hypocrites!* Does not each of you on the Sabbath untie his ox or his donkey from the manger, and lead it away to give it water? And ought not this woman, a daughter of Abraham whom Satan bound for eighteen long years, to be set free from this bondage on the Sabbath day?" When he said this all his *opponents* were put to shame; and the entire crowd was rejoicing at all the wonderful things that he was doing.

JESUS HEALS A WOMAN

REFLECTION

Doesn't it seem strange to you that when you perform a good deed, others sometimes try to make you feel bad about it? Here's an example: One day you see someone being bullied, and you decide to help that person, but you yourself end up being insulted and criticized. The bully might say, "Who do you think you are? Mind your own business! This is between this person and me."

What should you do? You can think about how Jesus handled such a situation. Jesus saw the crippled woman and decided to help her. He cured her, and what did Jesus get for performing a good deed? He received criticism. If you want to follow Jesus' example you must continue doing good even when you are criticized. Worry only about the welfare of the person you are trying to help, and not about what others will say or think about you.

PRAYER

Lord, when I witness a situation that needs my help, empower me to act in a way that would be beneficial to the person who needs my help.

Amen

JESUS HEALS A WOMAN
REVIEW

CHOOSE THE RIGHT ANSWER:

1. Jesus was teaching in one of the:
A. schools
B. synagogues
C. libraries

2. How would you describe this woman's ailment? She was:
A. bent over
B. unable to stand up straight
C. both

3. The leader of the synagogue was angry because:
A. Jesus partied on the Sabbath
B. Jesus rested on the Sabbath
C. Jesus cured a woman on the Sabbath

4. After Jesus cured the woman she began:
A. praising God
B. falling down
C. walking home

5. The opposite of opponents is:
A. friends
B. believers
C. enemies

JESUS HEALS A WOMAN
ARTWORK

Use your imagination to create a picture for this story.

DO NOT WORRY
LUKE 12:22-31

He said to his disciples, "Therefore I tell you, do not worry about your life, what you will eat, or what you will wear. For life is more than food, and the body more than clothing. Consider the *ravens*: they neither sow nor reap, they have neither storehouses nor barn, and yet God feeds them. Of how much more value are you than the birds! And can any of you by worrying add a single hour to your span of life? If then you are not able to do so small a thing as that, why do you worry about the rest? Consider the lilies, how they grow: they neither toil nor spin; yet I tell you, even *Solomon* in all his glory was not clothed as one of these. But if God so clothes the grass of the field, which is alive today and tomorrow is thrown into the oven, how much more will he clothe you - you of little faith! And do not keep striving for what you are to eat and what you are to drink, and do not keep worrying. For it is the nations of the world that strive after all these things, and your Father knows that you need them. Instead, strive for his kingdom, and these things will be given to you as well."

DO NOT WORRY

REFLECTION

Consider the images Jesus used in this story! Ravens, birds, grass, lilies, fields, toil, sow, reap, storehouses, nations of the world, span of life, and kingdom. These images added so much life to what Jesus was telling the people. They could relate to what Jesus was telling them, because the words he used were the same ones that they themselves would use in their daily conversation.

When we reflect on Jesus' message, we see the truth in it. We worry all the time about everything, yet nature seems to work without worrying about anything. Jesus tells us we are more valuable to God than the things of nature. He keeps them. He sustains them, and he would do the same for us, but we have to set our priorities right first. We must seek God first, and then all the other things we need will be given to us. This does not give us permission to be lazy, and wish our needs will fall in our laps. No, we have responsibilities to work for what we want, but it would be easier if we work with God.

PRAYERS

Dear Jesus, help me to develop a good relationship with you, knowing that with you, all things will be possible.

Amen

DO NOT WORRY
REVIEW

CHOOSE THE RIGHT ANSWER:

1. Who or what is of more value to God?
A. birds
B. lilies
C. people

2. Can you add a single hour to your life span?
A. yes
B. no
C. I do not know

3. Toil has the same meaning as:
A. sleep soundly
B. work hard
C. rest awhile

4. Solomon in all his glory was not clothed as one of these:
A. lilies
B. roses
C. sunflowers

5. Someone who is striving is:
A. worrying
B. crying
C. trying very hard

DO NOT WORRY

ARTWORK

Use your imagination to create a picture for this story.

LEAVE HER ALONE
JOHN 12:1-8

Six days before the Passover, Jesus came to Beth.a-ny, the home of Laz.a-rus, whom he had raised from the dead. There they gave a dinner for him. Martha served, and Laz.a-rus was one of those at the table with him. Mary took a pound of costly perfume made of pure nard, anointed Jesus' feet, and wiped them with her hair. The house was filled with the fragrance of the perfume. But Judas Is-car.i-ot, one of the disciples (the one who was about to betray him), said, "Why was this perfume not sold for three hundred denarii and the money given to the poor?" (He said this not because he cared about the poor, but because he was a thief; he kept the common purse and used to steal what was put into it.) Jesus said, "Leave her alone. She bought it so that she might keep it for the day of my burial. You always have the poor with you, but you do not always have me."

LEAVE HER ALONE

REFLECTION

Mary loved Jesus and wanted to do something nice for him. She poured out her love for him. She anointed him to prepare him for his burial. Not long after this incident, Jesus was crucified; he died, and was buried.

You can not anoint Jesus' feet with costly perfume made of pure nard, but you can look for ways to express your love for Jesus by doing nice things to others, and when you do, think of it as doing it to Jesus himself. Show kindness to your friend who decides not to talk to you anymore? Be respectful to the person who complains about you? Show love to the person who refused to help you clean out your desk? Share your stickers with friends who did not let you use their pencils? Congratulate your enemies on their successes? If you are able to show love to all these persons, regardless of what they did to you, then you will be showing just as much love for Jesus as Mary did.

PRAYER

My dear Jesus, help me to love you with my whole heart and my neighbor as myself.

Amen

LEAVE HER ALONE

REVIEW

CHOOSE THE RIGHT ANSWER:

1. Jesus went to the home of:
A. Elizabeth
B. Peter
C. Lazarus

2. What miracle did Jesus perform for Lazarus?
A. Jesus restored Lazarus' sight
B. Jesus raised Lazarus from the dead.
C. Jesus gave Lazarus many treasures from heaven.

3. Which one of the disciples is mentioned in the story?
A. Matthew
B. Judas
C. Peter

4. Did Judas really care about the poor?
A. yes
B. no
C. I am not sure

5. Someone who is poor is:
A. needy
B. satisfied
C. wealthy

LEAVE HER ALONE

ARTWORK

Use your imagination to create a picture for this story.

THE DEATH OF JESUS
JOHN 19:28-37

Later, knowing that all was now completed, and so that the Scripture would be fulfilled, Jesus said, "I am thirsty." A jar with vinegar was there, so they soaked a sponge in it, put the sponge on a stalk of the hyssop plant, and lifted it to Jesus' lips. When he had received the drink, Jesus said, "It is finished." With that, he bowed his head and gave up his spirit. Now it was the day of preparation, and the next day was to be a special Sabbath. Because the Jews did not want the bodies left on the crosses during the Sabbath, they asked Pilate to have the legs broken and the bodies taken down. The soldiers therefore came and broke the legs of the first man who had been crucified with Jesus, and then those of the other. But when they came to Jesus and found that he was already dead, they did not break his legs. Instead one of the soldiers pierced Jesus' side with a spear, bringing a sudden flow of blood and water. The man who saw it has given *testimony*, and his testimony is true. He knows that he tells the truth, and he testifies so that you also may believe. These things happened so that the scripture would be fulfilled: "Not one of his bones will be broken," and, as another scripture says, "They will look on the one they have pierced."

THE DEATH OF JESUS
REFLECTION

Jesus hung on the cross for about three hours. That was a very long time for someone to endure the pain of crucifixion. His last words were, "IT IS FINISHED." With that, he bowed his head and gave up his spirit. He had accomplished what he came to earth to do. He came to give his life as a sacrifice for our sins. We can truly say, "He accomplished his mission!"

Jesus' disciples felt very sad and lonely after his death and burial. They were full of grief, and disappointment. They had hoped that he was the one who would have delivered them from the bondage of the Romans who were occupying their land. Now that he was dead and buried, they felt they had nothing to

hope for. They could say, "He let us down!"

However, Jesus laid down his life for us. He said, "For this reason the Father loves me, because I lay down my life in order to take it up again. No one takes it from me, but I lay it down of my own accord. I have the power to lay it down, and I have power to take it up again. I have received this command from my Father." (John 10:17-18)

PRAYER

Dear Jesus, help me to die to things that draw me away from you.

Amen

THE DEATH OF JESUS
REVIEW

CHOOSE THE RIGHT ANSWERS:

1. What was Jesus offered to drink?
A. water
B. vinegar
C. wine

2. After receiving the drink Jesus said?
A. it is finished
B. it is over
C. thank you.

3. Fill in the blank. Jesus died on--------------.
A. Pentecost
B. Good Friday
C. Holy Saturday

4. What flowed out of Jesus' side after it was pierced?
A. water
B. blood
C. both

5. Jesus' bones were not broken.
A. true
B. false
C. I am not sure

THE DEATH OF JESUS
ARTWORK

Use your imagination to create a picture for this story.

THE RESURRECTION
MARK 16: 1-8

Mary Mag-da-lene, and Mary, the mother of James, and Sa-lo-me bought spices, so that they might go and anoint him. And very early on the first day of the week, when the sun had risen, they went to the tomb. They had been saying to one another, "Who will roll away the stone for us from the entrance to the tomb?" When they looked up, they saw that the stone, which was very large, had already been rolled back. As they entered the tomb, they saw a young man, dressed in a white robe, sitting on the right side; and they were alarmed. But he said to them, "Do not be alarmed; you are looking for Jesus of Nazareth, who was crucified. He has been raised; he is not here. Look, there is the place they laid him. But go, tell his disciples and Peter that he is going ahead of you to Galilee; there you will see him, just as he told you." So they went out and fled from the tomb, for terror and amazement had seized them; and they said nothing to anyone, for they were afraid.

THE RESURRECTION
REFLECTION

The resurrection of Jesus is the most significant event in the Christian world. Yes, it might surprise you to know that although there is great celebration at Christmas, Jesus' birth is not the most significant event in his life. It is his resurrection! Rising three days after his death and burial, is proof that Jesus is God, the Son of God. His resurrection gave him victory over sin, death, hell, and the devil.

Our faith tells us that Good Friday, the day on which Jesus died, was a sad day for his friends; but soon after Good Friday came the peace and joy of Easter Sunday. The story relates that some women went in search of Jesus on Easter Sunday, and they received the good news from a young man dressed in a white robe. He spoke these familiar words to them, "You are looking for Jesus of Nazareth, who was crucified. He has been raised; he is not here." (Mark 16: 6)

PRAYER

Dear God, help me to appreciate all that Jesus did for me. I know that Easter is a time of peace and joy, grant that I may experience that peace and joy every day of my life.

Amen

THE RESURRECTION
REVIEW

CHOOSE THE RIGHT ANSWER:

1. The women were looking for
A. Mary
B. Joseph
C. Jesus

2. What blocked the entrance to the tomb?
A. a branch
B. a stone
C. a car

3. Who rolled away the stone?
A. Mary
B. James
C. neither of them

4. According to the young man, Jesus was heading to:
A. Galilee
B. Bethlehem
C. Rome

5. Someone who is alarmed is:
A. silent
B. threatened
C. frightened

THE RESURRECTION
ARTWORK

Use your imagination to create a picture for this story.

JESUS AND THOMAS
JOHN 20: 24-29

But Thomas (who was called the Twin) one of the twelve, was not with them when Jesus came. So the other disciples told him, "We have seen the Lord." But he said to them, "Unless I see the mark of the nails in his hands, and put my finger in the mark of the nails and my hand in his side, I will not believe." A week later his disciples were again in the house and Thomas was with them. Although the doors were shut, Jesus came and stood among them and said, "Peace be with you." Then he said to Thomas, "Put your finger here and see my hands. Reach out your hand and put it in my side. Do not doubt, but believe." Thomas answered him, "My Lord and my God!" Jesus said to him, "Have you believed because you have seen me? Blessed are those who have not seen and yet have come to believe."

JESUS AND THOMAS

REFLECTION

Thomas was one of Jesus' students. He sat in Jesus' classroom for three years. During classes, Jesus taught him about the Resurrection, but Thomas did not listen, so when Jesus' words came true, Thomas could not believe. He wanted proof. Jesus showed his patience for his student by giving him the proof he wanted. Thomas responded in a very dramatic way. The story says that he answered, "My Lord and my God."

Sometimes we too behave like Thomas. We have to see and feel before we can believe. Here is a great opportunity for us to develop our faith in Jesus. He said that he would rise from the dead and he kept his word. There are many other things Jesus said he would do, look out for him to keep his promises. Jesus called us blessed, because we have not seen and yet we have believed. Are you one of the blessed, or do you need proof to believe in Jesus?

PRAYER

Jesus, like Thomas I declare, "My Lord and my God!" I believe in you.

Amen

JESUS AND THOMAS
REVIEW

CHOOSE THE RIGHT ANSWER:

1. Thomas was a:
A. musician
B. fisherman
C. disciple of Jesus

2. How did Thomas hear about Jesus' Resurrection?
A. he saw it on TV
B. he read about it in the newspaper
C. the other disciples told him.

3. Before Thomas could accept the fact that Jesus rose from the dead he wanted to
A. see the marks of the nails in his hands
B. put his finger in the marks of the nail and his hand in Jesus' side
C. all of the above

4. Jesus provided the proof Thomas needed by showing him:
A. his wounds
B. his tomb
C. his cross

5. Someone who is a disciple helps spread another's:
A. blanket
B. table
C. teaching

JESUS AND THOMAS
ARTWORK

Use your imagination to create a picture for this story.

FAREWELL AND ASCENSION
THE ACTS OF THE APOSTLES 1:6-11

So when they had come together, they asked him, "Lord, is this the time when you will restore the kingdom to Israel?" He replied, "It is not for you to know the times or periods that the Father has set by his own authority. But you will receive power when the Holy Spirit has come upon you; and you will be my witnesses in Jerusalem, in all Judea and Samaria, and to the ends of the earth."

When he had said this, as they were watching, he was lifted up, and a cloud took him out of their sight. While he was going and they were gazing up towards heaven, suddenly two men in white robes stood by them. They said, "Men of Galilee, why do you stand looking up towards heaven? This Jesus, who has been taken up into heaven, will come in the same way as you saw him go into heaven."

FAREWELL AND ASCENSION
REFLECTION

It was time for Jesus to leave earth and return to heaven. His three years of teaching had come to an end, and now he has to leave his friends without a teacher. How disappointing! His disciples still could not understand his teaching, or his message. They had expected a political Savior who would have rid their country of the Romans and restore the kingdom to Israel. Now that they realize that he was not that kind of Savior, they were filled with uncertainty. What were they going to do now? Who would be their leader now? Where was he going? Is he coming back?

The disciples had difficulty believing and understanding Jesus' teaching. It can be difficult for us as well. There are many things that we ourselves do not understand, and find it difficult to speak about, but as Jesus said in John 20: 29 "Because you have seen me Thomas you have believed, blessed are those who have not seen and yet have believed." We are among the blessed who have not seen Jesus and yet have believed.

PRAYERS

Jesus, give me the grace to tell the good news to all of my friends.

Amen

FAREWELL AND ASCENSION
REVIEW

CHOOSE THE RIGHT ANSWER:

1. Jesus' disciples were expecting him to restore the kingdom to:
A. Palestine
B. Israel
C. Egyptians

2. The disciples received power from the Hoy Spirit, and proclaimed the Good News in:
A. Jerusalem and Judea
B. Samaria, and to the ends of the earth
C. all of the above

3. After Jesus was lifted up what took him away?
A. a cloud
B. a wind
C. a waterfall

4. Where was Jesus going?
A. Israel
B. Egypt
C. heaven

5. To restore is to:
A. give back
B. return
C. both

FAREWELL AND ASCENSION
ARTWORK

Use your imagination to create a picture for this story.

THE HOLY SPIRIT COMES
ACTS 2:1-17

When the day of *Pentecost* had come, they were all together in one place. And suddenly from heaven there came a sound like the rush of a violent wind, and it filled the entire house where they were sitting. Divided tongues, as of fire, appeared among them, and a tongue rested on each of them. All of them were filled with the Holy Spirit and began to speak in other languages, as the Spirit gave them ability. Now there were devout Jews from every nation under heaven living in Jerusalem. And at this sound the crowd gathered and was bewildered, because each one heard them speaking in the native language of each. Amazed and astonished, they asked, "Are not all these who are speaking Galileans? And how is it that we hear, each of us, in our own native language? Par-thi-ans, Medes, E-lam-ites, and residents of Mes-o-po-ta-mi-a, Judea and Cap-pa-do-ci-a, Pon-tus and Asia, Phryg-i-a and Pam-phyl-i-a, Egypt and parts of Lib-ya belonging to Cy-re-ne, and visitors from Rome, both Jews and *proselytes*, Cre-tans and Arabs - in our own languages we hear them speaking about God's deeds of power." All were amazed and perplexed, saying to one another, "What does this mean?" But others *sneered* and said, "They are filled with new wine."

THE HOLY SPIRIT COMES

REFLECTION

Jesus knew that his disciples would be very sad when he left them. He knew that they would not have the strength or the courage to carry on without him. So he ordered them to stay in Jerusalem until he sent them a helper. They obeyed and went to the room, and they devoted themselves to prayer. Ten days later, the helper, the Holy Spirit came, and the disciples received power to become witnesses for Jesus. With boldness and courage they spoke the good news and baptized the people of God.

Teachers have an important job to do whether they teach Math, English, History or Science. If they do it well, their students will be prepared for the challenges of higher learning and a career. Those whom God calls to spread His Word also have an important job to do. If priests, evangelists, and prophets do a good job of teaching the Word of God, then their students will get the wisdom, understanding and knowledge they need to navigate the challenges of this life,

and hopefully find meaning and happiness in life.

PRAYER

Holy Spirit fill me with your grace and lead me towards wisdom, understanding and knowledge.

Amen

THE HOLY SPIRIT COMES
REVIEW

CHOOSE THE RIGHT ANSWER:

1. What advanced signal did the Holy Spirit send?
A. a sound
B. a call
C. a laugh

2. The sound was like the rush of a violent:
A. wave
B. wind
C. breeze

3. Everyone was filled with:
A. new wine
B. fresh water
C. the Holy Spirit

4. The disciples spoke about God's deeds of power.
A. True
B. False
C. I do not know

5. Someone who is bewildered is:
A. hungry
B. angry
C. confused

THE HOLY SPIRIT COMES

ARTWORK

Use your imagination to create a picture for this story.

PETER HEALS A LAME PERSON
ACTS 3:1-10

One day Peter and John were going up to the temple at the hour of prayer, at three o'clock in the afternoon. And a man lame from birth was being carried in. People would lay him daily at the gate of the temple called the Beautiful Gate so that he could ask for alms from those entering the temple. When he saw Peter and John about to go into the temple, he asked them for alms. Peter looked intently at him, as did John, and said, "Look at us." And he fixed his attention on them, expecting to receive something from them, but Peter said, "I have no silver or gold, but what I have I give you; in the name of Jesus Christ of Nazareth, stand up and walk." And he took him by the right hand and raised him up; and immediately his feet and ankles were made strong. Jumping up, he stood and began to walk, and entered the temple with them, walking and leaping and praising God. All the people saw him walking and praising God, and they recognized him as the one who used to sit and ask for alms at the Beautiful Gate of the temple; and they were filled with wonder and amazement at what had happened to him.

PETER HEALS A LAME PERSON

REFLECTION

When the lame man saw Peter and John, he was glad. He must have thought that surely these men would have a lot of money. But they did not have any; no money, no silver and no gold. They did not have what he wanted, but they did have what he needed. Peter had the power given to him by Jesus, and he used that power to help the man get up and walk.

There are many people who are in need of various things everyday of their lives and we can try our best to help even if we don't have much for ourselves. We can help with whatever means are available to us. We may not have money to give to those in need, but we can help them when we bring nonperishable goods to school or Food Banks to share with the needy. We help when we make and send cards to those who are suffering. We help when we smile and light up someone else's life. Above all, we help when we show compassion, love, and care.

PRAYER

Loving God, help me to reach out to the needy by sharing what I have.

Amen

PETER HEALS A LAME PERSON
REVIEW

CHOOSE THE RIGHT ANSWER:

1.　Why were Peter and John going up to the temple?
A.　to teach
B.　to eat
C.　to pray

2.　The lame man lay daily at the gate of the:
A.　palace
B.　church
C.　temple

3.　What did the man expect to receive from Peter and Paul?
A.　clothes
B.　money
C.　food

4.　The man was cured in the name of Jesus Christ.
A.　true
B.　false
C.　I do not know

5.　The man showed his gratitude by:
A.　crying
B.　laughing
C.　praising God

PETER HEALS A LAME PERSON
ARTWORK

Use your imagination to create a picture for this story.

RULES FOR THE NEW LIFE
EPHESIANS 4:25-32, 5:1-2

So then, putting away all falsehood let all of us speak the truth to our neighbors, for we are members of one another. Be angry but do not sin; do not let the sun go down on your anger, and do not make room for the devil. Thieves must give up stealing; rather let them labor and work honestly with their own hands, so as to have something to share with the needy. Let no evil talk come out of your mouths, but only what is useful for building up, as there is need, so that your words may give grace to those who hear. And do not grieve the Holy Spirit of God, with which you were marked with a seal for the day of redemption. Put away from you all bitterness and wrath and anger and wrangling and slander, together with all malice, and be kind to one another, tenderhearted, forgiving one another, as God in Christ has forgiven you. Therefore be imitators of God, as beloved children, and live in love, as Christ loved us and gave himself up for us, a fragrant offering and sacrifice to God.

RULES FOR THE NEW LIFE
REFLECTION

Rules for the new life is part of a letter Paul wrote to the people of Ephesus. In his letter, Paul calls on the Ephesians and all of us to make a new start. Those who follow these rules for the new life will be rewarded. Among these new rules are some lessons that you can begin to work on immediately.

1. Speak the truth.
2. Be kind and loving to all.
4. Treat others with respect.
5. Do not seek revenge.

These rules are not easy to keep, but if we practice them daily, they will become easier to keep. This will lead to harmony in our communities. God wants all of us to live in love, and everyday He gives us many opportunities to show others the love that is within us.

PRAYER

Lord Jesus, give me the courage to grow in this new life. Lead me to choose to do what is right in your sight, and help me treat my friends with love and respect.

Amen

RULES FOR THE NEW LIFE
REVIEW

CHOOSE THE RIGHT ANSWER:

1. The new life calls us to speak:
A. the truth
B. falsehood
C. tricks

2. What kind of talk should come out of our mouths?
A. curses
B. what is useful
C. evil

3. Let us put away all bitterness and:
A. anger
B. wrath
C. both

4. Someone who is tenderhearted is:
A. greedy
B. troublesome
C. full of love and pity

5. To labor is to:
A. work
B. lie down
C. rest

RULES FOR THE NEW LIFE
ARTWORK

Use your imagination to create a picture for this story.

A GOOD SOLDIER OF CHRIST
2 Timothy 2:1-7, 22-26

You then, my child, be strong in the grace that is in Christ Jesus; and what you have heard from me through many witnesses entrust to faithful people who will be able to teach others as well. Share in suffering like a good soldier of Christ Jesus. No one serving in the army gets entangled in everyday affairs; the soldier's aim is to please the enlisting officer. And in the case of an athlete, no one is crowned without competing according to the rules. It is the farmer who does the work who ought to have the first share of the crops. Think over what I say, for the Lord will give you understanding in all things. Shun youthful passions and pursue *righteousness*, faith, love, and peace along with those who call on the Lord from a pure heart. Have nothing to do with stupid and senseless *controversies*; you know that they breed quarrels. And the Lord's servants must not be quarrelsome but kindly to everyone, an apt teacher, patient, correcting opponents with gentleness. God may perhaps grant that they will repent and come to know the truth, and that they may escape from the snare of the devil, having been held captive by him to do his will.

A GOOD SOLDIER OF CHRIST

REFLECTION

In this story, the Apostle Paul brings before our minds images of the soldier, the athlete, and the farmer - people we know. Also we see other images of child, youth, witnesses, teacher, people, army, fight, crown, rules, and work. This looks like a story that we can understand. Paul tells us to be strong, not depending on our big muscles or our big size, but in the grace of Christ Jesus. We are called to be like good soldiers, good athletes, and good farmers.

We cannot let bad things; bad thoughts or bad people distract us from our goal. We are to be witnesses for Jesus, teach others, share in sufferings, and uphold what is right, faithful, loving, and true. Yes, we are to play our part and play it well according to the rules. Love God and love our neighbor. In the end, like good athletes, who played according to the rules, we will win our crowns, too.

PRAYER

Lord Jesus remain in me, and together we will be able to do great things. I want to be a good soldier in your army and fight the good fight.

Amen

A GOOD SOLDIER OF CHRIST
REVIEW

CHOOSE THE RIGHT WORD:

1. In what does a good soldier of Christ share?
A. prizes
B. suffering
C. Jesus

2. Athletes who compete according to the rules will be:
A. punished
B. scored
C. crowned

3. Do not be quarrelsome, be kind to whom?
A. everyone
B. no one
C. everything

4. When giving corrections to others, do so with:
A. anger
B. hatred
C. gentleness

5. Someone who is apt is:
A. gifted
B. clever
C. both

A GOOD SOLDIER OF CHRIST

ARTWORK

Use your imagination to create a picture for this story.

GOD IS LOVE
1 JOHN 4:7-13, 19-21

Beloved, let us love one another, because love is from God; everyone who loves is born of God and knows God. Whoever does not love does not know God, for God is love. God's love was revealed among us in this way: God sent his only Son into the world so that we might live through him. In this is love, not that we loved God but that he loved us and sent his only Son to be the *atoning sacrifice* for our sins. Beloved, since God loved us so much, we also ought to love one another. No one has ever seen God; if we love one another, God lives in us, and his love is perfected in us. By this we know that we abide in him and he in us, because he has given us of his Spirit. We love because he first loved us. Those who say, "I love God," and hate their brothers and sisters, are liars; for those who do not love a brother or sister whom they have seen, cannot love God whom they have not seen. The commandment we have from him is this: those who love God must love their brothers and sisters also.

GOD IS LOVE
REFLECTION

It would seem as if John wanted to make sure that all who read this story received his message of LOVE. The word love (s), (ed), appears more than twenty times in this story. How important is that four-letter word? It is very important. Love is an important ingredient in a relationship.

How is your relationship with God? Is it full of love? How is your relationship with people? Is it full of love? A person, who truly loves, is kind, respectful, compassionate, patient, understanding, forgiving, caring, polite and generous. Sometimes in our effort to find love we look in all the wrong places, and we find disappointment instead. Only with God can we find the God-kind of love. God is love. God is the only one who can truly satisfy our need for love. It is very easy to love those who love us, but how difficult it is for us to love those

who do not love us, or do not deserve our love!

PRAYER

Lord God, how can I say that I love you, when I hate others? Give me the grace to think about others, and be kind and generous in my dealings with them.

Amen

GOD IS LOVE

REVIEW

CHOOSE THE RIGHT ANSWER:

1.   Since God loves us so much, we ought to love:
A.   one another
B.   no one
C.   any thing

2.   Finish this sentence. God is ----------:
A.   love
B.   brothers and sisters
C.   fear

3.   What casts out fear?
A.   perfect love
B.   doubt
C.   crying

4.   Those who love God, also love brothers and sisters.
A.   true
B.   false
C.   I am not sure

5.   Someone who testifies:
A.   tells
B.   hears
C.   sees

GOD IS LOVE

ARTWORK

Use your imagination to create a picture for this story.

MICHAEL DEFEATS THE DRAGON
REVELATION 12: 7-12, 13, 17

And war broke out in heaven; *Michael* and his angels fought against the dragon. The dragon and his angels fought back, but they were defeated, and there was no longer any place for them in heaven. The great dragon was thrown down, that ancient serpent, who is called the Devil and Satan, the deceiver of the whole world - he was thrown down to the earth, and his angels were thrown down with him. Then I heard a loud voice in heaven, proclaiming, "Now have come the salvation and the power and the kingdom of our God and the authority of his Messiah, for the accuser of our comrades has been thrown down, who accuses them day and night before our God. But they have conquered him by the blood of the Lamb and by the word of their testimony, for they did not cling to life even in the face of death. Rejoice then, you heavens and those who dwell in them!" So when the dragon saw that he had been thrown down to the earth, he pursued the woman who had given birth to the male child. But the woman was given the two wings of the great eagle, so that she could fly from the serpent into the wilderness, Then the dragon was angry with the woman, and went off to make war on the rest of her children, those who keep the commandments of God and hold the testimony of Jesus.

MICHAEL DEFEATS THE DRAGON
REFLECTION

Even today, the war against good and evil continues to be fought. The enemy is known by several names, he is called Devil, Satan, Lucifer, The Deceiver and Father of Lies. Each of these names refers to the same evil spirit. He spreads terrorism, violence, and division in the hearts of God's people.

We must support Michael's team. We must be ready to fight the righteous battle against evil. Using our obedience and our good deeds, we can resist the temptations to do evil, even though it is all around us. Jesus our Savior will give us the power, the strength, the courage and the determination to choose good rather than evil. He has already shed his blood to redeem us from the hands of Satan. We must spread his message. Have no fear, we will win the battle! In the end good will triumph over evil. Bravo!

PRAYER

God, our Father, deliver us from evil and keep us in your loving care. Give us the grace to do good and resist evil.

Amen

MICHAEL DEFEATS THE DRAGON
REVIEW

Choose the right answer:

1. This story began in:
A. heaven
B. earth
C. the sea

2. Michael and his angels fought against the:
A. robbers
B. soldiers
C. dragon

3. The dragon and his angels were defeated.
A. true
B. I do not know
C. false

4. Another word for comrades is:
A. enemies
B. companions
C. dragons

5. Someone who is defeated is a:
A. winner
B. loser
C. conqueror

MICHAEL DEFEATS THE DRAGON

ARTWORK

Use your imagination to create a picture for this story.

ANSWERS

A VISIT FROM AN ANGEL:	1. B	2. C	3. B	4. A	5. C
BORN IN BETHLEHEM:	1. C	2. C	3. C	4. A	5. A
BOY JESUS IN THE TEMPLE:	1. C	2. C	3. B	4. B	5. C
JESUS IS TEMPTED:	1. C	2. A	3. A	4. A	5. A
FOLLOW ME:	1. C	2. B	3. C	4. B	5. A
CANA OF GALILEE:	1. B	2. C	3. A	4. A	5. C
JESUS AND ZACCHAEUS:	1. A	2. B	3. B	4. C	5. C
IS THIS THE CHRIST?	1. B	2. B	3. A	4. B	5. B
JESUS FEEDS THE CROWD:	1. C	2. B	3. B	4. A	5. A
JESUS HEALS BARTIMAEUS:	1: A	2. A	3. C	4. B	5. A
THE GOOD SHEPHERD:	1: C	2. B	3. A	4. C	5. B
THE CHILDREN'S FRIEND:	1: B	2. B	3. A	4. B	5. B
JESUS WALKS ON WATER:	1: B	2. A	3. B	4. B	5. B
JESUS IS REJECTED:	1: B	2. B	3. A	4. C	5. C
A GIRL IS RESTORED TO LIFE:	1: B	2. B	3. C	4. A	5. A
THE RICH YOUNG MAN:	1: A	2. A	3. B	4. A	5. A
LABORERS IN THE VINEYARD:	1: C	2. A	3. C	4. B	5. A
NICODEMUS VISITS JESUS:	1: B	2. C	3. C	4. C	5. B
JESUS HEALS A WOMAN:	1: B	2. C	3. C	4. A	5. A
DO NOT WORRY:	1: C	2. B	3. B	4. A	5. C
LEAVE HER ALONE:	1: C	2. B	3. B	4. B	5. A
THE DEATH OF JESUS:	1. B	2. A	3. B	4. C	5. A
THE RESURRECTION:	1. C	2. B	3. C	4. A	5. C
JESUS AND THOMAS:	1: C	2. C	3. C	4. A	5. C
FAREWELL AND ASCENSION:	1: B	2. C	3. A	4. C	5. C
THE HOLY SPIRIT COMES:	1: A	2. B	3. C	4. A	5. C
PETER HEALS A LAME PERSON:	1: C	2. C	3. B	4. A	5. C

ANSWERS

RULES FOR THE NEW LIFE:	1: A	2. B	3. C	4. C	5. A
A GOOD SOLDIER OF CHRIST:	1: B	2. C	3. A	4. C	5. C
GOD IS LOVE:	1: A	2. A	3. A	4. A	5. A
MICHAEL DEFEATS DRAGON:	1: A	2. C	3. A	4: B	5. B

MINI-DICTIONARY

Abraham: a friend of God; ancestor of a multitude of nations

accord: of one's own free will; by one's own choice; willingly; voluntarily

adultery: unfaithfulness to the marriage vows, usually committed by married people.

ailment: an illness

ancestors: family members who were born even before grandparents

apt: just right for what is being said or done; appropriate, clever

atoning sacrifice: Jesus' gift of his life on the Cross to pay for the sins.

battered: to beat or pound with great noise

common (purse): belonging equally to everyone

conceive: when a woman becomes pregnant with a baby

controversies: arguments and disagreements

denarii: Roman money; payment to laborers for their work.

despise: to dislike very much

eternal life: life that will go on and on; life that will last forever; salvation

favored: to show like or approval of

Galilee: the area around the Sea of Galilee where Jesus grew up, preached, and did most of his miracles.

hired men: workers; laborers who perform services for pay.

hypocrites: persons who pretend to be good or religious without really being so.

indignant: angry about something that does not seem to be fair

inferior (wine): not so good (wine)

MINI-DICTIONARY

Jerusalem: the most important Jewish city in Bible Times.

Jordan: a country in the Middle East, east of Israel

manger: a box in a stable where food is place for the animals

Messiah: the person God promised to send to save the people from their sins.

Michael: Chief angel; one of God's chief messengers to men and women.

nard: pleasant - smelling oil made from the roots of spikenard plant.

opponents: those who are against others in a fight, contest, or debate.

Passover: a feast in memory of the freeing of the Jews from slavery in Egypt.

Pentecost: A Jewish feast celebrated 50 days after Passover; in the Christian Church, this same feast is celebrated 50 days after Easter.

Pharisee: a Jew in the time of Jesus who strived to obey every part of the Jewish law.

pinnacle: the highest point (of the Temple)

prophet: a religious leader who people believe speaks for God.

proselytes: new believers; converts to the Christian faith

Rabbi: a teacher of the Jewish law; a leader of a Jewish congregation.

ravens: large, black crows

registered: to list one's name in a register or book.

righteousness: thinking and doing what is right; fair, just, and holy

scroll: a long strip of paper or parchment, usually with writing on it.

MINI-DICTIONARY

sneered: mocking or funny remarks to hurt someone's feelings

Solomon: a wise king of Israel; son of King David

stature: the height of a person.

sternly: strict or harsh; without gentleness or tenderness

steward: a person who looks after the comfort of customers, and serves food and drink.

synagogue: a building where Jews gather for worship and religious studies.

temple: a permanent place in Jerusalem where the Jews worshipped God.

testimony: giving proof that something is true.

womb: the part of a woman's body in which a baby grows before birth.

wrangling: to argue in an angry noisy way

wrath: very great anger

ABOUT THE AUTHOR

Claudette Francis (B.Ed. McGill University) entered the teaching profession in September 1954. For more than half a century, she challenged students to work hard and reach their God-given potential.

Francis was born in Guyana, South America. She left her country for Canada on Sunday July 20th the same day that American astronauts landed on the moon. Living and teaching in Canada, gave her the opportunity to continue in her calling as an instructor of God's Word. She made good use of drama to help her students understand Biblical stories, and satisfy their hunger and thirst for spiritual nourishment.

Francis is now retired from active classroom teaching. Nevertheless, she hopes that her deep faith in God and lively commitment to Jesus will continue to inspire God's people, as she continues to do her part to fulfill Jesus' commission: "Go into all the world and proclaim the good news to the whole creation." *Mark 16:15*

ABOUT THE ARTIST

Barbara Richardson was born in England, and served as a nurse in the 2nd World War. She immigrated to Canada in April 1954 aboard the ship called "United States of America."

Richardson continued her career as a senior nurse in the East General Hospital Maternity Ward. She enjoyed many interests which included singing in the choir at Trinity Anglican Church. She had a great love for painting as evidenced in her painting on the front cover of this book. I painted this picture as if a child had painted it, with the thought in mind that children would be able to relate to it," said Richardson.